n*e*

Being The One

As well as being a poet, Sarah Littlefeather Demick is a freelance respite carer. She works mostly with people who have dementia, working alone. The powerful and revealing poems in this collection are mainly born of Sarah's work. They illustrate her feelings about the people and situations she encounters every day, usually in social isolation or confinement. Others reflect the reality of the person who provides that care, the reality, emotions and experiences of that person seen as the 'carer' who is also a poet.

Sarah Littlefeather Demick is an Ojibwa Indian who was born in Canada but raised in the UK by adopted English parents. She lives on a farm in Cumbria.

Also by Sarah Littlefeather Demick

Another Creature (poetry, 2016)

BEING THE ONE

Sarah Littlefeather Demick

Naked Eye Publishing

© Sarah Littlefeather Demick 2022

Book design and typesetting by Naked Eye

Cover illustration: Robin Ross

ISBN: 9781910981252

www.nakedeyepublishing.co.uk

Acknowledgements

Thanks to everyone who has lived with me through the writing of all these poems. Most especially, my thanks and love always to Rod, Gary Booth, the Whytes, Jennifer Copley, Smalls, and to everyone in my work world.

The poem *tips for being a carer* previously appeared in *Poetry Review*.

Sarah Littlefeather Demick

BEING THE ONE

For Ros and my uncle, Lol

Contents

Introduction

Part I

Part II

Introduction

I AM A FREELANCE RESPITE CARER. I work mostly with people who have dementia. I work alone. I am employed by private individuals who find me through word-of-mouth, by reputation. I sometimes need to respond to advertisements and attend interviews. I am often without work. I am often away from home. Some work has lasted years, others months or weeks, and very occasionally, only hours. "I couldn't do your job" is often said to me by people who imagine what my job is.

It seems to me, firstly, that you think I have some kind of extraordinary capacity for patience. In fact, I do not possess more patience than anyone else and I am often in situations where I can hear the dust settling and would tear out my own fingernails if it helped to speed things up – waiting for an answer, or some kind of reaction, to a question, a direction, or a suggestion. Often a question which has been asked many times. And often a question which has been asked several times in the immediate past e.g. "would you like a cup of tea?"

Often though, the question relates to a specific and extraordinary support need: specific, as in helping someone to put their tights on (for example) and extraordinary perhaps, because they could do it by themselves yesterday but need help today. And saying something like "now put your foot in" isn't always helpful if that person has forgotten what their foot is, or how to put it in. Or 'in' what? So I have to examine that person closely, find out where the problem is, and think of a way to sort it out. With tights – sometimes, if you get one foot in, the other magically 'remembers' what to do, and they go on, automatically. Sometimes it's best to forget about wearing tights that day – especially, if after a couple of hours, they're still not going on. And sometimes it's best not to ask questions at all. With the cup of tea scenario – I usually just make one anyway.

So, my job – being a carer – is not just about patience. It's about encountering individual human problems and working out ways of solving them. It's about recognising that these problems will present themselves – if they have not already done so – and that people affected, cannot solve them alone. It is also not just about the practicalities of problem-solving but the complex and demanding emotional side-effects for people who need help: It is often hard for anyone to give themselves up to care, but it's hardest for those who have always been otherwise independent, capable, and fortunate. And that's probably most people.

Then there's the projected horror of, say, needing someone to help you eat your food, help you get undressed, help you in or out of the bath/shower – or the imagined absolute nightmare of needing someone to help you go to the toilet. It's so horrific, you can barely ever bring yourselves to say or think it. But if you are in need of such specific help, isn't it lucky that there is someone capable and willing to do it? And not only that, but they will also do it with good grace and expertise.

I say, 'imagined absolute horror' of intervention on a close personal level, because as humans we are not unused to closeness (with other people). Think of Turkish baths and hot tubbing, going for a massage, a haircut or a manicure, or hugging and kissing, or the peculiarities of the sex act. We are naturally gregarious and geared towards partnering, but the difference with a carer is that they may not be your person of choice. And you may not have time for social niceties before intimacy. And that intimacy may be associated with unpleasantness, similar to medical (or dental) examinations and procedures, and you may experience embarrassment, frustration, or fear. And sometimes, entire rituals that used to be 'normal' must be modified or reinvented. Every day. Every hour.

Woman R (page 33) lived on a farm with a number of pets, who were all called 'Poppy'. She had been struggling with dementia for several years and needed help with daily living but was otherwise physically healthy. Several other carers attended in rotation. Her dementia had progressed so far that she no longer understood spoken language, so instruction/direction had to be explicit by clear tonal expression and mime. Our morning routine was consistently and emphatically traumatic because she did not understand the need to shower (she had nocturnal urinary incontinence) and she did not understand instructions for how to get into the shower – which, unhelpfully, was in a cold bathroom and over the bath (so, one had to step into, then stand in, the bath). The process often took up to an hour and Woman R would be cold, frightened and angry. The same process for me was stressful, tiring and guilt-inducing.

I first became a carer when I was about eleven or twelve years old, when my father became seriously ill. He was diabetic and suffered bouts of debilitating illness for about two years before he died, aged just forty. As the eldest of three daughters, with a mother out at work, the task of care sometimes fell to me. I was mostly terrified. Later, I helped care for my grandmother, who'd had a hip replacement and needed help during her recovery. I went to stay at her flat in North London, I seem to remember it was for a few weeks, and took my dog with me. I cooked meals, helped her with transfers from bed to chair, and helped her to have a shower. I also remember that she was catheterised and the smell of the rubber hose lingers with me yet. I was mostly terrified in this circumstance too, and worried about doing things 'correctly'.

My first 'proper' job was as a Houseparent (I don't think that title is used anymore) in a children's home – having thought I'd try it for a while until I decided what I really wanted to do for a living. It turned out that what I really wanted to do, and seemed to have a knack for, was to help people with extraordinary problems to live ordinary lives. And maybe that's what you mean, when you say, "I couldn't do your job". I suspect that you probably just don't want to. It is not lucrative, the hours are long and antisocial, and you will often be unwelcome in your place of work. Other professionals – even within the care industry – will look down on you. There is no kudos. And yet, paradoxically, speaking to ordinary folk who are wives, husbands, parents, children, brothers, sisters, or neighbours, if you are caring for one of their own – there is much kudos.

The poems in the collection are born of my life in this country and in this job, as a woman of Native American heritage. I have grown up deeply valuing our bond with nature and the spirituality of my heritage may be evident in my poems, whether they are about my work (part I) or the rest of my life (part II).

The poems in Part I are about the people and situations I encounter every day who are usually living in situations of social isolation or confinement, and they are intended to illustrate the way I feel about my work. My intention in sharing this with you is that you understand a little better. And if you understand a little better you might want to, or be able to, respond a little more confidently to people in your community who experience life in a different way from you. Other carers may do things differently and other carers may not be interested in being accountable. This is my experience. And as a reader, you are my witness.

Sarah Littlefeather Demick

I

an explanation

i am required to give affirmation and comfort
most of the time
i am required to be human
all of the time
with particular emphasis on laughing
and if you ask
why we are laughing
we probably won't be able to explain it
and if we could
you probably wouldn't be able
to understand
because you are sailing in a world
where rationality is hung from the
masts of society and culture
while we are afloat elsewhere
regularly beached in a place we don't recognise
or one we must recreate everyday
so forgive us
if we throw back our heads
and howl

?

you looked at me
from the other side
of the abyss
the desert of your mind
and echoing through the
fading light
like tumbleweed it came
your question
what happened to me
                    ?

life and time
the answer stood there with us
in the hallway

aye
life and time

to my successor or one who comes in my stead

when you come to work, leave your life at home.

learn patience! nothing will be accomplished by hurrying. sometimes things will take longer than they did before, and sometimes you will be knuckle-grindingly frustrated by waiting in situations where you can practically hear hair growing.

sometimes things will take even longer than that.

practice humility. nothing is about you. you are in service.

do not be competitive, complacent or loud.

read carl rogers and practise the provision of unconditional positive regard towards your charge. it is an art but you can learn it.

all practical tasks should be done the way your charge desires. not the way you would do.

in short, be the perfect carer and if you can't be the perfect carer you must put on the performance of being one.

all day and every day.

and often, part of the night.

then you may go home and in the same way you might throw a shawl around your cold shoulders, you can reclaim your own life.

night shift

I won't mention *dignity* or *death*
instead I give you
ephemera and *oeuvre*
I may even try euphoria and freedom
and I'll not say *prayers* or *sympathy*

but hear me
as I whisper this into the dark
           I am with her
         the song of her
         the bowl of her
         the whole of her
and now
      the nearly gone of her

things that can happen (when you're a carer)

your charge will forget your name and may call you kathy
kathy may be the name of another carer who does everything
better than you

the gardener (who has approx. 10 mins face-to-face time with
your charge on a fortnightly basis) may tell you how best to do
your job

your charge may ask you what time it is (and you say, 10
o'clock, or whatever it is)
and then they'll say *why* is it 10 o'clock

your charge may try to change channels on the tv with the
phone

or

try to answer a ringing tone by saying hello hello hello into the
tv remote control

you may be wittered at from a distance

you may be wittered at from close quarters

incessantly

when there is a break in wittering – you may wonder if you
should call a doctor or an ambulance

always check for breathing first

you may suffer from stress-induced headache or backache

you may suffer sleeplessness

you may wish you'd chosen another job

you may wish you'd chosen another life

A Random Half Hour

We are 'watching' The Return of the Pink Panther. My charge
has poor eyesight and therefore limited ability to watch
anything. Especially anything on TV. I have already noticed
that Christopher Plummer is in this film, and who
coincidentally, we have seen in a couple of things this week
already.

You're not going to tell me that's Christopher Plummer! She
exclaims triumphantly when another actor is in close-up on the
screen.

No. That's Herbert Lom.

Oh, I don't know what I'm going to do about Kathy, she
continues, ignoring me and referring to a received but
unthanked-for present. Of two vests.

Herbert Lom, meanwhile, seems to be experiencing some kind
of traumatic discomfort at the mention of the name 'Clouseau'.

I hate getting clothes as presents. Don't you?

She doesn't wait for my answer.

I keep telling my daughter-in-law.

She rings Kathy (eventually. The first time, she's accidentally
put the mute switch on, so there's a lot of hello-ing at our end).
She thanks her for the lovely vests. Which, incidentally, are
unworn and of no interest, even tho' they are exactly the same
as the ones she loves and wears all the time. Which were a
present from the daughter-in-law. And which, she tells me,
were from Harrods (but say M&S on the label).

28

Then we look for her glasses. Which, it is suggested, I have misplaced. She attempts to start going upstairs, where the glasses may have been left by the kettle. There is some dramatic staggering and lunging at furniture to hold on to (while a Zimmer-frame stands idly nearby). I intervene and go upstairs to look. They are nowhere in sight. They are eventually found in her handbag. Where they have been since last night's trip to the doctor's surgery. Where she herself put them.

Then we look for today's papers (having found the glasses, one can read the paper). Which she's sitting on.

I find myself transmogrified into Herbert Lom.

in her mind

time is on a loop
and it was quiet
when she asked me
the question
is he dead?
yes, i replied
is it permanent?

again, there was silence
enough to hear hair grow

interloper

i've always wanted to belong in a family
i've tried several
but they didn't fit me
most of them were too tight

so now i go away
to try to belong
in someone else's family
for a week or so, every month or so

it's perfect
i get to belong
but i get to leave
before they find out who i am

as a carer

i am no pushover
i will bestow polite tolerance
for the way life has made you
but there is a bold
and deferential line
that should be recognised
from both sides
i do not expect you to do more
than you are able
and – unless you have dementia –
i expect you to do the same for me
and when it comes time
for the exchange of money for services
i ask you to remember
you are buying my time
and expertise
but not my respect

Woman R

whose mind was mired in demented thoughts, could not understand how to get dressed in the morning. Every morning. One day, this little conundrum was becoming a scenario where we were achieving less getting dressed but significantly more getting frustrated and upset. I suddenly discovered that a desperate human response was a helpful answer to our predicament – so when I finally burst into tears, she responded towards me with affection and generosity.

Then she helped me
to help her
to get dressed that day.

.

a summer morning with (and for) Man T

there's a whisper of lazy clouds
like dancing swans
above a thousand gently rasping bovine molars
and a secret morning hare
who knows we're here

later, we watch
from the kitchen sink
the red-rumped woodpecker
and the decorated goldfinch
with her whirring wheedling fledglings

while the lonnen disappears quietly
into a dark hole at the far end
and the long june daylight hours
softly woo the stately iris
and the laughing, waving poppies

i tried to make this poem with
sanctus hubertus
and the little fans of your ginkgo tree
but the animals wouldn't let them in
so i've had to leave them out

in the morning

poor old trout
doesn't want a bath
but by the time it's run
and we've spidered
(four legs and a zimmer frame)
along the hallway
from the bedroom
and i say
in casual surprise
oh look – your bath is ready
she gets in happily
forgetting she didn't want it

kissing gates

surprisingly tricky

an agony
of negotiation
and juxtaposition

had us beat

my charge

She is short of memory, vision, patience, tolerance, and empathy. But at 94 years old, she is also short of time. We make do with my ability to know what day it is, to open cellophane packets, and any other useful qualities I can conjure from experience.

She likes sugar, ice cream, syrup, and cake. She pretends to like dark chocolate but really prefers milk.

She likes walking round the garden and telling me all about how hard she worked to transform it from a field to the verdant dance of spring it is now. She would probably never use the word 'verdant'.

She brags endlessly about her family. It is clear who the favourite is.

She has outlived most of her friends and thinks she may have been forgotten by death.

She is suspicious and doesn't trust easily. She is used to doing things her own way. But she follows me around and I sense her need. For company and someone capable. Somewhere during the week she has decided I am PLU (People Like Us).

I am not PLH (People Like Her). I know this because I write poetry that doesn't rhyme. I have a tattoo. I never eat salad cream. I sleep in a different room from my husband and I allow dogs on the bed.

But I am a good actor: I pretend to be PLH (but still never eat salad cream).

By the end of the week we are old friends.

the horses of the demented mind

click their dancing hooves up and down the road of change
i try to bridle them but they pull away
with my fingers caught in their manes and my hands too weak
to grip
the horses of the demented mind
shatter memories in a rodeo of time and dust
they know which way the wind blows and where the water falls
but never share secrets from their velvet mouths

when they know what i do for a living

of course
in answer to your question
i have professional patience
but i am not
by nature
a patient person
unless of course you count the years
i waited patiently
for the anxiousness of youth to dispel
or my mother to say she was proud of me
or my first husband to stop wishing i was thinner
that was a lot of years
but patience
eventually
landed in my life
like frost in a field
on a spring morning
and i learned that patience is not the same as waiting
patience is more peculiar than that
patience is hard to get hold of
patience is a balancing act
between yesterday and tomorrow

caring for Woman C

life moves into a slower sense
and talk of death
is braided into conversation
like you'd already left
even the potting shed is lonely
and the garden tended by another
i covet the little green picture next to your bed
with its indistinct figures hiding in the shadows
and notice that time is
rapacious now
for small details and distant memories

after a birthday

the circling year
paused for breath
and counted bluetits
nuthatches and woodpeckers
in the garden that day

you kept saying
you couldn't see the point
in not dying (after all this time)

it seemed clear
the tunnels and secret chambers
in life's ante-room
were still full of temptation and curiosity

the unravelling

for you
will be different
from the unravelling
of anyone you know
or selves from other places

as you were revealed
extraordinarily
from the bricks of time
mortared with dreams
and loves' lichens
hidden in the dust of your walls
in the undoing
ruin and fossil will know your name
uniquely
and you may not need us anymore
for all the things you used to

it will not be laming
but kaizen
if there's courage
to see it that way

and we'll be left
sifting memories like old clothes
some will be outgrown
or cast

and some will be cherished
with no knowing
of who will do the cherishing
or why

tips for being a carer

it doesn't matter
what kind of madness is evident
you've just got to get them
safely and happily
through the next hour or day

doing the right thing
isn't always possible
and is sometimes futile
but apathy is abhorrent

wear friendly clothes

learn and practise humility
then do it some more.

Being The One (putting George to bed and other things no one knows)

We need for you to make the transition from day into night.

I lead you by the hand while talking in tones of positivity. I steer you to the bedroom where the lights are turned down low and I explain what we are going to do. You don't understand and you bridle. But you relent eventually. Enough for me to gently peel off your jacket and deftly, like a magician, make it gone (I've thrown it under the bed). And you forget you were wearing it. We likewise disappear the tie and waistcoat. And I talk to you like I used to when I was helping the farrier shoe a wild horse – holding your attention with my eyes and soothing with my voice. While your resistance is low, we slough shirtsleeves. And as you begin to recognise something is happening – I have already slipped you into the coolness of a neatly pressed pyjama-top and you fasten the buttons with fumbly fingers. As you are doing that, I loosen your belt and start to remove your trousers, then leading our strange dance, I turn you so you can sit on the edge of the bed. And then I am kneeling in front of you like Mary of Bethany. And you are talking to me and telling me something you want me know but I never will. In the next few moments we pull the pyjama bottoms up and my power has restored safeness in your world. And you say 'oh darling you are the one'. And we are both happy. Encouraging you to lie down, I start closing down the night for you. And I kiss you goodnight.

I always kiss you goodnight.

II

allow yourself

to think about things
in a different way
stand by the lake
and see how the water
knows the shore
and if you learn
that a desert
of grief and turpitude
must be journeyed
then allow yourself
to be swallowed whole
by the vermilion sunset
and go to the other side
loose your heart to the skies

flying tiger

it's an open-ended puzzle
intruding on the sky
it is might and speed and danger
streamlined in a dreamscape
the eagle
is a closed drawer
keeping its secrets
to itself

uprooted

i see you in dreams of the past
and remember loving you
with an open-necked heart
and you just left

i see you again
in winter's cold water
and grey skies
where you once sheltered me
in rabbit fur and smoke
and then left me again

and when at last
in the deepest crimson swell of lust
you took the very last pinch of me
i ripped out my own roots
and set myself adrift

a day on the farm (at lambing time)

my shepherd
coaxes life from the fellside
onto the fellside
over and running through
the fellside
hungering for helios
while the verdant dance of spring
is illusive
mischievous
courting death
with a frosty breath
on doomwatch
killjoy

at the point of the bayonet with Doctor Bolton

he opened an eight-year
conversation
with one question

and i gave him
all the answers
i ever had

which amounted to
various shades of nothing
and the spaces in between

his patience was a staging ground
for my sorrows and their
blind and raging loneliness

and being in the same room
with him
was all i ever needed.

my father

you put down your glass
and walked into the trees
you recreated yourself
as bird and flew
to the uppermost boughs
of those same trees
and sit there
even today
while i write
and feel your gaze
on my back
like warm sunshine
and i listen for your song
but it never comes

i lied

about how much i loved you
as we lay on my fur coat
in the snow
when i had freewheelin' belief
in almost everything
you said to me
and i thought destiny
might see us through
but my hands bled
from tumbling in gravel
and there were friction burns
on my wrists
and i didn't care
because you'd given me
an hour of bliss

you were everyman
you were nothing

a review of my life as tulips

i like it when the leaves droop
when they no longer have the strength
to stand up
cos i've been there
i like it when bob dylan
plays those old songs again
and i like it when we watch a film
but can't remember
if we've already seen it
i like it when the roads are quiet
i like it when i can type as fast as i think
i like your line about power cables
draped over the countryside
and clouds being like lines of fortune
on the hand of god
i like having a map of greenwich
where i can see it everyday
i like crispy sweet apples
that laugh before they fall
i like dogs' ears
and how they feel like velvet
and how in the early days
near bear point in fact
we were so attracted to each other
the stars and the grass knew it
and that night we sat in the park
and you wouldn't touch me
and i wouldn't let you anyway
and when i did
all the rules for everything
were written and broken again
with no thought for the universe

and i remember that i probably never played guitar for you
and you were never faithful
but i believed your desperation
hell
it nailed me to the floor
like the first time you said you loved me

godless for a while

so, god, unable to reconcile their self
to the way things had become
(after humanity had so polluted the world
with hatred and indifference)
allowed their self to sulk

and in that dark and tainted space
they learned to accept their own frailty
they learned to embrace the sorrow
to own the anger
and to wallow in broken dreams

and when at last they felt like coming back
they tried to love harder
and with more music than before

and so it was easier
for them to be to be found
(by seekers and needers)
and they stood on mountain tops
and riverbanks
they laid out flowers
along the lakeshores
and made it warmer
in the forests
and in the oceans

aubade for a golden retriever

when i breathed your air
i breathed the air of grasses and clouds
i breathed the air of woodpeckers
and badgers and my lungs were filled
with all of life at the behest of my nose
and the earth had a way
of cocooning my feet
and holding me in its spell
especially if rain was falling
and especially when rain fell
we walked in the woods together
until i saw you run on ahead
and in your nature
gone

i see your shadow in the trees sometimes
and the sun reflecting on the tips of your ears
and your goodbye is there edged in pale fawn fluff
and the haze of another new day

the beck as love (for otter)

i recognised the beck as love
it was rushing
it was hurtling
while i tried to stand my ground
to contemplate the changes in my life
it was the taste of slate and hardship
it was the slip of danger
it was the only way to travel
and the one best avoided
it was inevitability
it was nothing to do with love
it was everything to do with love
it was a verse of you
and the haunting refrain
of the world without you
it was us all over

a poem for RTD

if i wrote a poem about you
the words 'astonishing' or 'extraordinary'
might not be in it
unless I think of the time
it took us about two hours
to walk home from a pub
that was less than half a mile away
or the resounding mayhem of dog-gigs
or you landing on your knees
at one hundred miles an hour
for air-guitar solos in the centurion
(or ever imagining that one of my poems
would contain the word 'centurion')

if I wrote a poem about you
it would be about sex in the shower
or watching you work
under the bonnet of an old rover
it would be about fags and lager
and the pervasive smell
of axel grease and leather
it would be about meeting you
at the crossroads
between your house and mine
and your life and mine
and it might have your friend sean in it
who was astonishing and extraordinary

smile

when it first appeared
my smile was boundless and full
it was fascinated by sunsets
and the sound of arpeggios from my father's guitar

then the years multiplied like molehills
and the only music left to me
was hanging in cobwebs

i put my smile away in a box
and bought a cheap replica from the rag and bone man
(who'd found a job lot
outside the pub on the corner of our street)
and now i wear that one
most of the time
my birth smile stays in its box
and keeps itself busy
playing old records of julian bream and segovia

throwing shadows

my arms are spliced into rope
and wrapped round the neck of a large dog
who is brave and gentle
but clumsy in unexpected ways
and bound to each other
we bark at things that frighten us
and create fear where it wasn't before
we howl at creatures in the night
making our own song
but cause sleeping birds to fall out of trees
landing on their backs
and their feet throw shadows
that look like daffodils emerging
i am not
who you think i am

now you're gone

i saw you pushing against a high wind
your perpendicular alignment was out of true
you hugged your sheep and cattle around you
as if you were frightened they might blow off
with your hat and coat
i was not there

i was not there again
in the vision of life
where you and the dogs
barbecued a feast of marshmallows
on the lakeshore in summer
and the dusky sky was alight with flies and embers

but i was there
in the run-off from the slaughterhouse
with the carcasses of crippled families

a warning

the north wind took time out
from roiling over the oceans
and sat down beside her
it said – little girl don't go looking for love
where it first doesn't introduce itself
and most especially
don't drink in bars
don't do it for days at a time
your true self will not flower there
although people will know your name
and heads will turn
nakedness will be imagined
in ways you will never understand
and sculpted from their cold cold need
they will become etched on your body
some people
will want to keep you
and some will just want you
to paper over their imperfections
with your sweetness – watch out!
they will take it from you

i measure days

without you in birds
see how little garden finches
soon become loons and divers
with their long black shadows
mirrored on the lake
i measure sadness
by putting stones in a jar
like the crow in a story
my mother used to read
and i measure love
with sleeping dogs
and wild cherries

listen

to the sunshine
falling through the trees
like ancient coins
and see how cobwebs
hold lost dreams and heartache
listen to the suck
of feet in sand
and laughing flights of curlews
see how the shoreline
belongs to all worlds
and how my voice
always
mines a seam of loneliness
that echoes in your night

dear poem fairy

if i can go to the place where the poems are
(as i've oft heard you explain)
why isn't it in the same place twice?
i know you said something
about learning and honing
but you never told me
there may only ever be one
one
poem
that truly wants to be found
or captured
and now i realise also
that i must find that place
in the dimension of wild reason
and make some room
for that line or stanza to emerge
and then
i must allow myself to align with it
if i'm to exist at all

yours faithfully and evermore

on poetry

because i am bipedal
i may accompany you on your journey
as any other friend
but my quest is multi-footed
and by day
fleet as wild mustangs on the open prairie
and by the fall of night
predates through language
like a pack of hungry hyenas
feasting on the stark beauty
of naked verbs
and the perilous persiflage of philosophy

fifteen

you said the marsh-girl
in a coral-coloured book
reminded you of me
i read it too
and was reminded of myself
i remember the losing
the waiting, the desperation
and the loneliness
i remember birds and feathers
shells and sand
i remember the lakeshore
and the seashore
and wondered why it wasn't
called the oceanshore

that loneliness, Jennifer

was palpable
and wholehearted
sometimes it was bird
sometimes it was stone
it was the marrow in our bones
and the sound of boot heels
staggering and weaving
down corridors of rhyme
but because it was scattered
and sown in the way you describe
it was like this for all of us

Santorini

an apricot sun melted into the ocean
where seahorses grazed
and reared their young to be mindful
of typhoons, tsunamis
or the jump of predation
hidden in the waves

black sand between my toes
the glass and the grist
the back of your hand

i never went there again

routed

i do not want to smell like food
so i do not smear my body
with coconut oil or vanilla
i do not like to use
the word 'shard'
but sometimes you have to compromise
and i do not like to find you
repeatedly
in my past and in my dreams
where your enchantment
holds me ransom to myself

i still don't believe you
and i demand
to be set free

the swallow

will take you over fields
and through dreamscapes
in the clouds
but never in the forests
where the trees
shake out their branches
like fishing nets or parasols

what if

i'd been born to you and not gifted from a stranger
what if i'd worn the right smile all my life
and not the one I pasted on
that looked like confidence or defiance
what if i'd known how to ask the right questions
what if i hadn't failed to raise your awareness
to my fear and anxiety
and i'd been able to tell you everything
what if i'd told you i didn't know how to live
and the mistakes i was making were crippling me
what if you'd noticed and changed the order
of daughters who needed you

and what if our last conversation
is the conversation we are not having

a poem with no mothers

memories will not come cresting over the hill
nor will i run out to meet them if they were
singing, as i might other heroes of time
no, my childhood remembrances
will be dredged from ocean depths
where a slim shaft of light, glinting like polished copper,
will signify their whereabouts and be their only comfort

the memories will not come
for they are fastened to their point in history
on the boating pond at greenwich park
or skidding down the hill in front of general wolfe
and laughing in the wind
theirs is the echo of foghorns on the river
and through the masts of the cutty sark
theirs is the shadow of the city
falling on parched pavements at lovell's wharf

they will not be met or known
search for them yourself
look through the lens of time and hold your head just so
you may glimpse the fading outline of a pre-pubescent girl
walking to church with her father
or not looking back
as she is swallowed by the yawn of the school gates

this poem is not funny

you'd be more likely
than anyone
to know all about
how i should get things done
and which character
in any poem might be the 'i'
and which nouns would best suit
the 'you'
but no idea
about how
some people
sometimes
have to break the week into seasons
and decide if wearing sweatpants
is summery or autumnal
or pick their fingernails
til they bleed lucid lyrics
or sceptical anthropomorphisms
about children
taking revenge on their parents
and how
now i'm sixty-five at last
i am learning to gyre in the sunset like a salmon

pandemic dream (no.1)

what was it a picture of exactly
was it the tiny ships
or the long taut ropes
or was it the easy stride
through waist-deep water of
the coronavirus as gulliver

how the world is changed!
and how difficult to determine
that which is real
from the stuff of dreams.
but this is what I saw:
the continents drawn together
and moving in the same direction
dragged by their prows
as gulliver's ears grew deaf
to the commands of
their lilliputian crew
and the backdrop
is clouds-on-blue-sky
(in a turner-esque kind of way)
and the noise that's rising
is baleful strings and kettledrums
orchestral haze
to block all else

the children playing
the sirens screaming

and gulliver wades on

on moving home for the 93rd time

i would not be taken aback if my teddy bears,
who i've just packed into a spacious and warm cardboard box,
decided not to move from this barnlife
but chose instead
to stay in the lovely south facing room
where a curlicue of bats in the summer
decorated the worldview
and we forgot about demanding women
who want what they want,
when they want it
because they pay the wages
bugger it!
let me get in the box with the bears

before i do tho'
my friend jenny
advises writing a poem about everything
so, i pick up my pen and try to write
about adventures and hightimes
and how i've seen the whole country
flowing downhill from the north to the south
as if it's falling into the channel
and i try to keep from thinking
about how my father and some animals on tv
came home to die

St Crispian

for the first time
since moving to cambridge
the moon is shining through the trees
(and not just behind them)
and something later revealed
is that st crispian was a twin

by the river

i will not be the one to see it
but i will have noticed
that not all things
rolling under the bridge
have fallen from the same cloud
and i might be thinking about
sycophantic ghosts
with their splinters of guile
and i'll be glad it was you
who saw the kingfisher

the last poem

the last poem of the year
fell from the curtains
and spilled onto the stage
like a moonlit waif

in the hollow of the night
the last poem of the year
faltered over its lines
but made it to the end

Naked Eye Publishing
A fresh approach

Naked Eye Publishing is five years in existence and still fledgling: an independent not-for-profit micro-press intent on publishing quality poetry and literature.

A particular focus is literature in translation. We aim to take a midwife role in facilitating the translation of works that have until now been disregarded by English-language publishing. We will be happy if we function purely as an initial stepping-stone both for overlooked writers and first-time literary translators.

Each of us at Naked Eye is a volunteer, competent and professional in our work practice, and not intending to make a profit for the press. We see ourselves as part of the revolution in book publishing, embodying the newly levelled playing field, sidestepping the publishing establishment to produce beautiful books at an affordable price with writers gaining maximum benefit from sales.

nakedeyepublishing.co.uk

CPSIA information can be obtained
at www.ICGtesting.com
Printed in the USA
LVHW081150271022
731543LV00013B/529